I0558871

THE WRITING MACHINE

(Writings on Writing: Occasional Ruminations On an Intangible Legerdemain)

Greg Bachar

Books By Greg Bachar

The Amusement Park of The Mind
2013

The Writing Machine
2013

The Sun Poems
2016

The Book of Was
2017

Advanced Studies in the Rocket Absurd
(2023)

THE WRITING MACHINE

(Writings on Writing: Occasional Ruminations On an Intangible Legerdemain)

Greg Bachar

Rowhouse Press 2013

To Mom, for our lifelong dialogue about writing.

Acknowledgments

"Love & Books in the U-District," appeared in *Tablet*. "The Only Manifesto Is the Blank Page" appeared in *The Capilano Review*.

Cover by Greg Bachar.

THE WRITING MACHINE

PROLOGUE

WRITING

AN ORGY OF WRITING

DISSONANCE & CACOPHONY

PROLOGUE

RIVETS, DUCKS, SWANS, LEEKS, MOTION

What do I know about writing? I'm not entirely sure. When I write, it's like breathing and although there are occasional "asthmatic blockages," it usually flows freely and with little thought.

So, by "not entirely sure," I don't mean that I don't know "things" about writing, just that the process of writing seems like such an intangible legerdemain that any attempt to try to explain it will also be an intangible legerdemain.

When I stop to think about writing or what I'm writing while I'm writing, it's usually to think of what I'm going to write next or to try to remember what I was going to write that popped into my head while I was writing but disappeared into the ether when I couldn't catch up to it.

These are small moments, though, that quickly pass, after which I return to The Zone. Perhaps I've been heavily influenced by the Surrealist concept of automatic writing, as it feels like most of what I've written has been written in a state of improvisation.

Perhaps the real writing process takes place later when I look at what needs fixing, editing, and revising. Case in point, the collection you now hold in your hands. These pieces accumulated over the years with no conscious plan of turning them into a book.

Future technologies, some of which are in the pipe already, such as computer-brain interfaces that might one day allow a person to think a piece of writing onto the page directly from their brain, will give us new things to talk and theorize about as far as writing is concerned.

For now, though, the conversation is one that is set in various pre-established topical modes, and I'm sure that this collection is no different.

I'm not sure writing can be taught. "Learned" is probably more accurate because, being an art form, it begs one to experiment with it so one can learn for themselves what they want their writing to be and what they want it to do.

As a creative act, writing is a rebellion against inactivity and mindlessness that requires one's active participation along with a heavy measure of self-teaching.

Writing is inherently psychedelic and embraces aspects of alchemy in that the physical object, the book that is held, read, and shared began as nothing but the energy of thought in the brain that left the writer's mind via the pen or keyboard and entered the reader's brain via the pages of the book. This is revolutionary technology at our disposal and yet we do so little of it when we aren't "required" to write.

Why?

It is much easier to consume than it is to create, to hit the power switch, flip through the channels, and let someone else's vision substitute for ours as the mind goes blank and the television light flickers and dances across our faces.

Take a picture of yourself watching television. Tack it to the wall near where you write. It should motivate you.

Writers write. This is the simple truth, if there is one, about the art form known as writing.

Whether the words you write on the page are rivets, ducks, swans, or leeks, what you're doing with these words is instigating thought, instigating action, reaction, and therefore setting things in motion.

Now it's your turn. Breathe.

MY MACHINE

My machine would do my writing for me. His name would be Mr. Machine. He would be made from steel. He would be a big machine. The color would be silver. The magic button would be on the side with the other buttons. I would not tell anybody about my magic machine.

THE ONLY MANIFESTO IS THE BLANK PAGE

WRITING

ASK THE WRITER

Setting ideas in "stone" on the page might lead a reader to think they are ideas the writer believes to be true.

As mentioned in the introduction to this volume, though, writing is an intangible legerdemain.

Any attempt to set ideas about writing in "stone" might win a game of rock, paper, scissors, but ideas are like wishes and wishes are fishes that can't be caught.

Ask yourself your own questions about writing and write your own answers you think to be true.

Years later you'll read them again and see how your ideas have changed or remained the same (or both).

DIFFICULTIES?

One obstacle is staying motivated to write. Another obstacle is making sure I use my time to write rather than doing other things.

Writers write. If you want to be the writer you dream of being, then you have to adhere to this simple fact.

Browsing books at a bookstore on any day other than Saturday (book browsing day) makes me want to get home as quickly as possible and work on my own writing.

All those books are a reminder of what I should really be doing with my time.

I usually carry a notebook, which allows me to work on writing projects when I am out and about, like "The Art of Pool."

For a whole summer, I kept a notebook in my pocket whenever I went out to play pool, which at the time was almost every night.

My goal was to learn everything I could about the game as if I was a beginning novice and to write a "how to" book about pool when I finished my apprenticeship. Whenever I thought I learned something new about the game I wrote down a simple, straightforward note to use as a springboard for ideas to be explored later.

Someday I'll sit down and synthesize all these little bits into their greater whole. It doesn't matter that I gathered these notes several years ago.

They are seeds I have stocked away for future plantings. Follow whatever writing vibe pulls you along at any given time.

The seeds will keep and ward off famine someday.

"GOOD" LITERATURE?

All forms of art are always in a state of flux and what we think is "good" changes from year to year as new advances are made.

What I think is a good literary work is different from what you or the next person thinks is a good literary work. Perhaps "good" literature is whatever sings to you alone.

That being said, there are forces in the literary world that dictate what is perceived to be "good" literature. Critics, reviewers, editors, and teachers pass on the literary canon from generation to generation. These writers' works are considered "essential" reading down through the ages that capture universal truths in the themes they address. There are many great writers and works of literature in the canon, but the work of many writers left off the list is often where the real action can be found.

My tastes change somewhat from phase to phase of my writing and reading life, but I have my own personal literary canon, and you should too. I don't read as much fiction as I used to. Reality seems stranger and more interesting. If you read the news every day you quickly see that reality invents stories no author could ever imagine.

Alive, the story of how people survived a plane crash in the Andes mountains; *The Great Escape*, about a daring and epic tunnel escape from a German P.O.W. camp in World War II; *Papillon*, the epic true story about a man falsely accused of murder and his subsequent escape attempt from Devil's Island; these and several others in a similar vein of people fighting against the odds have always provided me with literary solace and inspiration.

I could type up a list of author's names and books that, for me, represent "good" literature. You might enjoy discovering some of these books, but you probably have your own list, so perhaps the best thing to do is to carry a card in your wallet to distribute to people who ask you who your favorite writers are.

THE MOST IMPORTANT WRITING SKILLS?

The most important writing skills to have are a vision of what you are trying to create; the effect you want your creation to have on your readers; knowing how your writing fits or does not fit into the literary traditions that preceded you.

Another important writing skill to have is the ability to experiment and test your limits as a writer or the limits of the form of writing itself. Even if the experiment you perform has been done before, it will be new to you and might lead to some interesting pieces of writing.

Another important writing skill to have is the ability to embrace reckless abandon so as to throw yourself into your work with no thought given to any of the important skills mentioned above or that might be mentioned elsewhere.

Your writing is yours. You can be as gentle or as rough with your words as you want. They like to be tickled into new configurations and if your words are tickled then your readers might be tickled by them as well.

A final important writing skill to have is the ability to attempt to capture something epic in your work. Strive for the ability to show people things they haven't seen or thought they saw but didn't know how to put into words.

Last, and it's not even a skill at all: write.

WRITING, MOOD, & ALTERED STATES?

Since writing is done alone (you can write in a coffee shop or library surrounded by people, but it is still a solitary act), one's mood at the time of writing probably depends at least a little bit on how you feel about being alone.

There have been nights I've gotten back from having a great time and feel like getting some of the night down on the page. There are other nights when it felt, in the end, that my time would have been better spent staying home instead of going out in search of some kind of story.

Lately, I've been doing a lot more writing in the early morning. This is new to me. In person, I am grouchy in the morning, but on the page, I can achieve some clarity and get things done.

It would be interesting to know how and when each part of the books we read were written. Perhaps one line here on a bar napkin, a few chapters there written blandly at home as it rained outside, a chapter written in an airport terminal while resignedly waiting for one's snowed-in flight to be released for take off...

There have been quite a few fine and interesting books written over the years about writers who either wrote under the influence or enjoyed consuming various substances on a regular basis.

Some writers starting out might be left with the impression that indulging in some substance or another is a necessary key to unlocking the door of creativity. Nothing could be further from the truth.

Substances, whatever we're talking about here, might help one "see," in that they alter one's perception of the world in some small or overwhelming way, but I'm not sure they help facilitate the actual writing process itself. They might, though, give one the gift of visions seen while under their spell that one can then bring back to the page, but for the most part it seems like mixing the two rarely results in anything truly earth-shattering.

That being said, there is value in working one's mind, with or without assistance, into the state of "total derangement of the senses" poet Arthur Rimbaud referred to so that one's thoughts explode on the page and are not self-censored in any way.

A glass of wine will certainly help put one in a sort of trance state in which the words seem to spill from the fingers to the page with the same ease that the wine flowed from its glass into the mouth, but so will staying up late or getting up early to write when your mind is feeling sleepy.

So will exercise or deep breathing exercises that help to trigger the endorphins that are our body's naturally occurring opiates secreted after both physical and creative activity.

Some writers I've read happened to indulge in various substances, from beer to wine to heroine to psychedelics to speed, and some of them wrote about how they used these substances in a deliberate attempt to experiment with the creative process while being under the influence.

William S. Burroughs was the notorious Beat writer known mainly for his novels *Junky* (about being a junky) and *Naked Lunch* (written under the influence of junk). Jack Kerouac and Allen Ginsberg visited Burroughs when he was working on the latter and found him in a state of considerable disarray, the manuscript pages strewn all over his room. The two helped to assemble the manuscript and shape it into the book it would eventually become.

Burroughs also applied the cut-up method to the work by cutting each manuscript page into four squares and shuffling the squares around with other cut up pages from the manuscript, which were then assembled and re-typed in that cut-up form.

Burroughs later admitted that he had little recollection of writing the book, so immersed was he in junk at the time.

This is the same William Burroughs who, in a later interview about the narcotics and writing, said, "remember, anything that can be done chemically can be done in other ways."

Finally, there is the creative act itself. There is no greater narcotic than simply getting into the making of something. There's nothing better than a good writing binge just for the sake of going on a writing binge, at the end of which the floor is strewn with pages for you to mull over the next morning when you wake up and wonder what happened.

"What did I do?" you might ask, looking at the mess. You made something, and it was *free*.

WRITER'S BLOCK?

Repeat after me: "Writer's block does not exist." What you are really saying when you say you have "writer's block" is "I don't feel like writing." My advice to you about anything you don't feel like doing is this: don't do it. Do something else you want to do and then come back to writing when you "feel like it."

It's possible that the concept of "writer's block" comes from the misguided assumption that works of art arrive "pre-made." They don't. The creative process is messy and chaotic. Ninety per cent of writing is thinking. Ten per cent is the action sequence where you get your ideas down on the page. The rest is "postproduction" where you go back to edit and shape the "clay" you made into the finished form you want it to take.

One hears professionals in all fields talking about how important preparation is. With this in mind, doing the necessary prep work should help you ease away from the illusion known as "writer's block." Making lists and rough outlines are especially helpful.

Perhaps some writers expect a piece of writing to spill out onto the page in its final revised, polished form.

Sometimes this happens; you get into "the flow" and it's all there as if it was already written for you.

More often than not, though, whatever you first put down on the page is most likely a "demo" version of what will later become the final product. Editing and revising are not inherently exciting processes, but they are part of the creative process and require a greater attention to detail than the initial spark of creative activity. Regardless, repeat after me: "Writer's block does not exist."

LOCATION?

I can write pretty much anytime, anywhere. I am happiest with a Pentel Rolling Writer and yellow legal pad, but since the advent of the computer I've grown more comfortable with the keyboard, which helps to eliminate time spent typing handwritten work into digital form.

Sometimes I like music in the background, but it's not a necessity, though it can sometimes help to get into the necessary trance state. Sometimes the right background movie can serve the same purpose. I especially like French films in the background. Something about the sound of people speaking French is relaxing.

Sometimes I write in a small notebook whenever I get an idea that seems worthy of writing down. Sometimes I write on a cocktail napkin with a pawnshop pen and jukebox music blaring in the background while waiting for my turn at the pool table. For a writer, every moment is a potential writing moment, no matter where or when.

When I was in grad school at UMass, Amherst, I spent several days and nights each week at Amherst College's Robert Frost Library. I set myself up at a desk with whatever assigned essays I went there intending to work on, then I'd wander the stacks and pull down five or ten books to browse through that were completely unrelated to the assignment.

At some point, I walked outside and across the commons to the view spot and looked down at the soccer field, tennis courts, the woods below, and the hills in the distance. Sometimes I'd take a "break" and go to the coffee shop for a snack, then return to my desk. More browsing of books followed, more wandering of the stacks, and more discovery of new members of my literary family.

Sometimes I'd write something. Other times these library wanderings didn't incite writing until I got home later and fell onto the bed crouched over one of my notebooks.

When I worked as a weight room attendant in the UMass, Amherst recreation center one summer, I read for two hours, wrote for an hour or two, and lifted weights or shot hoops until the end of my shift.

I read and wrote A LOT that summer and worked myself into the best shape of my life, all in a humid thirty by thirty-foot cage occupied by people lifting weights, grunting, and sweating.

Sometimes it seems like I do my best writing anywhere else but home where there are always too many easy reasons to become distracted. Regardless, writers write, wherever they are. As my grad school friend and poet John Parker used to say, "lethargy is for the others."

BEGINNINGS?

A piece of writing has to start somewhere even if it starts in the middle of a sentence, like when you meet someone new after overhearing something they said that piqued your interest and you add a comment to the dialogue and get to know that person and suddenly they are your friend or more: where do those stories "begin?" When you look back on non-linear events, they appear as linear stories with definite beginnings and endings.

Every journey begins somewhere and ends somewhere else. I suggest from now on we refer to beginnings and endings as departures and arrivals because every journey takes you somewhere from which you end up back home again with a bag of souvenirs and a head full of memories.

A piece of writing is a souvenir. Remembering a piece of writing you read once means you went on a journey that took you somewhere and deposited you safely back where you started with the journey's story firmly embellished in your mind. In the words of the Japanese poet Basho: "The journey is home."

I'm not sure there is a "process" for beginnings. There are "processing" lines in factories, not on the page. On the other hand, I sit down and start writing or I am walking and think of a line and stop to write it down, or I am out on the town at a bar or coffee shop or restaurant or show and something comes into my head and I write it down or try to remember it to write down later so I can type it up or put it in the file where other such thoughts lay dormant until a day or two arrives each year when I have some time to go through the pile and pan the gold dust from the silt.

I once had the idea to start a poetry factory. It would look just like an industrial factory. "Workers" would be required to wear some kind of uniform, punch in, and write poetry in eight-hour shifts, twenty-four hours a day, unionized of course, with a one-hour break for lunch and two fifteen-minute breaks for brainstorming. The existing public market would dictate subject matter.

Custom poems would be written for customers who special ordered them. Soon, poetry factories would spring up all over the world, stock would be traded and sold, fortunes made and lost on the finicky nature of the poetry market. Oh, how I wish there was a poetry factory.

"B.S."?

"B.S." is only a term that con artists use. That being said, there is a connection between being a thief and being an artist. It's all about what you can get away with and how far you can push the limits without getting caught. A thief is an invisible "artist," though, while an artist or writer plies their trade in public for all to see.

The thing that should keep you from "B.S.'ing" is that everyone in the world possesses their own "B.S. Detector," and they are activated all the time.

Do we "B.S." our days? No. The better word is *improvisation*. We improvise all the time, but when we call it "B.S.'ing" we do a disservice to the very root of creativity: making something out of nothing.

What pushes you should be the goal of pure expression, the desire to capture moments in words, and the hope that you might create something unique, if not unique to the world, then unique to you and your experience of the world.

You might not be Picasso, but then, Picasso wasn't you.

FAME?

You will find your audience, or your audience will find you, or you will live a life of artistic obscurity, be "discovered" after you are gone, or NEVER be discovered. Regardless, the only thing that matters is the work and the doing of the work.

The sun is going to fade and finally snuff itself out. Write for those around you now. Write for those within reach. Write for yourself. Don't think about the future. Don't think about the sun.

IS IT GOOD FOR YOUR HEALTH?

Jogging, tennis, basketball, and cycling are good for the body. When you write, you sit for hours at a time crouched over a pad of paper or a computer screen. That can't be good for the body. A contented mind, though, can make the body happy, and if you are in creative overdrive all those parts come together.

Yesterday was my friend's birthday and everyone agreed to get dressed up. Another friend and I wore suits. After dinner downtown, we went back up to the hill for a nightcap and a game of pool at Linda's. It felt good to shoot pool wearing a suit and tie. My friend suggested we were playing better because of it. I agreed. Wearing the suit while shooting pool made my body feel more...something. I've never tried wearing a suit and tie to write; perhaps that will be my next experiment.

Tonight, I went out to shoot pool. I'm almost finished doing research for the book about pool, but each night I learn something new or at least a nuanced version of something I already learned.

A guy I played against last week showed up. He is young and full of attitude, has a nice girlfriend, is in law school, and is close to taking the bar exam. He appears to have his life in order. I thought he should have won each game he lost (he lost every game he played) because in each of those games he made one and only one poor decision that cost him the game. He lost the last game on a brilliant shot by his opponent, an almost impossible angle against the eight ball in the corner that clicked against the fifteen ball before going in. He shook his opponent's hand and decided to argue about it after the fact because, he admitted later, he didn't really see what had happened, but his friend told him the cue ball had tapped the fifteen.

I left wondering to myself what kind of lawyer this guy is going to make if a.) he is out on the town shooting pool instead of working on a case; b.) there is a relationship between how one shoots pool and how one leads one's creative life or career; c.) he overlooks one crucial detail in everything he does while still expecting to win.

Meanwhile, I played three off games, the first one after not eating all afternoon and during which my dinner arrived. The quickly eaten food rejuvenated me and though I found myself nearly down and out, my opponent having made all his shots but the eight ball and me having made none of my shots, I settled myself into a bit of a groove and started dropping nice, relaxed, smooth shots into the pockets. I was pretty sure I was going to win the game, in fact, I knew it. Or at least I knew what I had to do to win.

Looking back, though, I didn't slow myself down enough when shooting for the last stripe in the corner. It was an easy bank shot but I rushed it, and that turned out to be the game. I wasn't disappointed as it was my first game of the night, but at the same time, once I sat down in the chair of defeat and reflected on my mistakes, I realized that I should have won the game, especially when my opponent lost the next game so decisively.

What was even more telling was our handshake after the game. The guy's hand was sweaty and cold. He wanted to win that game badly and I took him right to the edge and almost broke him.

How does this relate to writing? When you play pool, you aren't really playing against an "opponent," you are playing against yourself. When you write, it's just you and the page. Which would you prefer: eight ball in the corner pocket of a game that no one but you will remember tomorrow or eight pages of your book that will exist forever? Unless that eight ball is worth a million dollars, the answer should be a gimme.

TIME TRAVEL?

Much of what we know about past cultures and distant history comes from the artifacts those cultures left behind. When the artifact is a piece of writing or a work of visual art, we can get a clearer, though still partial, picture about what that culture was like. When we write we are sending messages to the future to the long line of humanity that will come after us. Think about what you want to say.

WILL IT LAST?

In the grand scheme of the universe and human history, writing and print have only been around for a little blip of the whole timeline. At some point, language emerged, probably very basic at first but quickly growing more complicated as everything in the world needed to be named, and at some point, some primitive beings had the idea to paint and write what they saw on the walls of caves.

Early written communication took many different forms from what we know as writing today. Once handwriting emerged, books were first hand-written one at a time. Then the printing press was invented and for the first time a leaflet or tract or book could be produced on a mass scale, and everyone could own one for his or her home.

This process represented a radical shift in the evolution of consciousness and how we shared and received information. Information became something private, tailored for the individual.

If we look at the history of print, from the printing press to now, it's a little tiny blip in the evolution of communication. In a lecture he gave in Seattle, Terence McKenna suggested that we are currently witnessing print's demise and evolution into something else, something visual, and that if we look around, we can see much evidence of this. We're returning, as Marshall McLuhan wrote, to being visual creatures in an auditory world.

McKenna also stated that, "the world is made of language." This is a very simple but profound statement. Everything we do is dictated by language, be it thinking or speaking. We say, "I want a pizza" and the pizza arrives. We think, "what if we assembled this, this, and this, and threw in this?" and the nuclear bomb is born. Obviously, a simplistic rendition, but you get the point.

There will always be language, but language and forms of presentation will always be evolving. Maybe the answer to the question is really another question: what form will writing take in the future? If we could have a glimpse, we might not recognize what we see.

INSPIRATION?

Anything can be a source of inspiration. People say things all around us every day. Sometimes they are great sentences that these people have no intention of writing down, much less remember, so feel free to use them to set off a piece of your own work.

A friend of mine recently read a few of my absurd stories and said they "made no sense." I said, "What do you mean, they make no sense?" She said, "They're all like, a woman woke up with a nose made of butter" and we both laughed hard enough to spill some of our soup.

"Can I use that?" I asked.

"Sure," she said. She didn't realize the gold she'd just given me and now I've been walking around trying to figure out what to do with a woman whose nose is made of butter. All I can come up with so far is that she's looking for a man with a face made of bread.

Where is the rest? I haven't found it yet. At this point it is more like a puzzle or a mathematical equation: woman times nose made of butter plus man with face made of bread = ? I hope to figure it out soon.

I wish I could remember the lines of the story I was going to write once about the discovery of a light bulb farm a man discovers after climbing to the top of a hill, but I didn't write them down when they popped into my head, but without those lines that one is lost forever.

You never know when or where ideas will arrive. Always be prepared to capture them.

EMBARRASSMENT?

At some point in grad school, I started publishing and handing out collections of my writing. You can wait all your life to be "discovered" but if you're smart, you'll take a more D.I.Y. approach to get your stuff out there. Musicians do it. Painters do it. Why should there be a different standard for writers?

My first chapbook was a collection of four love poems I wrote while thinking about a woman I was infatuated with after seeing her around campus. I typed them up one after the other in about twenty minutes on my friend's typewriter while we were waiting for another friend to pick us up and drive us to the Amherst Alehouse for a round of beers.

I re-typed these four poems and assembled them into a pocket-sized chapbook called *Four with Crossed Fingers*. On the cover I pasted a Xerox of a World War II era photo of a man about to be executed. In the picture, he is tied to a pole and standing on a pile of sandbags.

Just a few feet in front of him is a row of riflemen pointing their weapons at him. I thought it was a great image that captured the feeling of wanting to say hello to a stranger you want to meet.

It's also an image that captures the feeling of sharing your writing with an outside audience. The only way to find out if others feel the same way about you as you do about them is to step up and see what happens.

The same goes for your writing. Get it out there.

IS QUALITY DECREASING?

There are fewer people, statistically, reading books and newspapers. At the same time, more people are reading and writing in all the various digital realms. Those who are interested in being writers will always find a way to be writers, though perhaps they will choose film, television, advertising, video games, computer programs, or new forms of expression and presentation.

And what if we are one day able to connect the brain to a computer with a program that allows one to transcribe their thoughts? Instant novels, without setting one drop of ink to the page. This is one of the most exciting times, creatively, to be alive. There are so many tools and channels for you to take your creativity into your own hands.

It's not a time to be cynical. It's a time to, in Terence McKenna's words, "put the art pedal to the metal."

AN ORGY OF WRITING

AN ORGY WITH AN ASTERISK

The pieces in this section were written when I was a graduate student in UMass, Amherst's M.F.A. Creative Writing Program taking Peter Elbow's Writing and Teaching of Writing course.

Although I was there to study fiction, the program had a hefty dose of required academic courses in addition to creative writing workshops that were designed to make the program "Ph.D. equivalent."

Elbow's course was supposed to prepare us for teaching composition to undergraduates while enrolled in the program, but he was as interested in exploring the writing process itself as he was the end results of that process.

He invited us, at the start of the quarter, to participate in "an orgy of writing" and wanted us to leave the course with a huge stack of writing about writing.

I completed fifty pages of free writing about the writing process in Elbow's class in addition to several required formal essays.

It being my first semester in graduate school along with the fact that there was only one other creative writing student in the class (everyone else was working towards Master's degrees in English and Composition Theory), I didn't feel entirely at home.

I didn't see the use at the time of talking about a process that seemed so intuitive and natural to me. I didn't feel a need to examine it, especially when a lot of the class dialogues, perhaps because most of the class were not creative writers themselves, seemed geared towards figuring out what writing "is."

With that in mind, perhaps myself and the one other creative writer in the class were the only ones who knew what to do: stop talking and write.

A lot of dialogues in the class made it seem that a lot of my classmates felt that writing was more like science or math rather than a form of art and creative expression. It seemed that there was a lot of energy invested in trying to narrow down the teaching of writing into a set of equations that would lead to a one size fits all teaching approach for every student regardless of their own specific needs and despite their own individual way of expressing themselves with words.

This is a simplistic and perhaps somewhat off base description of what was going on then in this regard (and is still going on now), but regardless, I did not go to grad school to be told how to write, to be told what writing "is," or how it "should" be taught.

I went to grad school to learn about literature by immersing myself in research, writing, and making friends with like-minded writers in the program.

All those things were accomplished then, so now, years later, it is interesting to confront my writings about writing from Elbow's course.

I don't agree with everything I wrote back then, and because we were required to turn in so many pages of writing about writing each week, I remember often feeling that I was just trying to fill pages to satisfy the requirement.

I don't know what to believe are my sincere ideas about writing at the time and what is page filler. With that in mind, this entire section of the book should be read with a big asterisk.

An orgy with an asterisk.

WHY WRITE?

The question of "why write?" has bent and twisted and melted into the possibly more direct and pertinent question of "write *what*?" as my thoughts have turned towards the kernel of the nut and away from broad and general vagueness. For the writer or the student of writing, it isn't so much a matter of deciding whether to write, but of finding a subject worth writing about. The fact that the student is in a writing class precludes the possibility of not writing. He or she must write to pass the class. And for the writer, he or she either writes or he or she does not exist as a writer, so the issue is the same for both: each is in a position where writing must and does, one way or another, in the short run or long, happen with more than irregularity. For the writer or the student of writing, writing is a given.

As writers, our frustrations often stem from a sense of the futile that is inherent in our work. Why write when we don't care about our writing? Why write when we are only writing for a teacher? Why write when there are an infinite number of more interesting things to do than sit in a room at a desk above blank pages and pour hollow words onto those blank pages when the words we really want to use elude our grasp and the things we really want to say we think we cannot say because it is an "assigned" essay?

The number of things that might take precedence over writing is infinite, if they are allowed to. Life, after all, is lived in the world, and writing is lived only on the page. The writer who is committed to writing for life must sacrifice various aspects of his or her daily existence in favor of the page, but it is not so easy for the student writer to make such sacrifices. For most student writers, writing is done in passing on the way from one place to someplace else where duty or reality calls (a.k.a. "good times") because not only is life filled with things that take precedence over writing out of necessity, it is also filled with things that *arc* more important (i.e. "good times").

If there is anything that student writers write for it is the assigned topic first, followed by the satisfaction of having conquered and completed writing about the assigned topic. Life consistently subverts our desires by forcing us to address the immediate and the necessary when what often matters most is the random, arbitrary and superfluous. The writer's dream of sculpting the great novel is pared down to meet reality's needs. Instead of writing what we want to write, we are given assignments that don't capture our imaginations. Bad topics are like bad jobs. The writer attends to them every day but complains all the way.

The issue, then, is subject matter, not necessarily the motivation to write. Just as there are certain books that we love to read and cannot put down, so too are there topics that we cannot stop writing about because they consume us. It takes little effort to read good writing. Often it feels the same way when we are writing something that we really enjoy writing about and is more fun than flogging away at someone else's soggy biscuit of a theme or assignment.

Case in point, the paper at hand, which is meant to be a loosely constructed research text somehow related to writing or the teaching of writing. Since I am not teaching yet, I've leaned towards the writing aspect of things for my subject matter. I initially selected a broad enough question (why write?) without any idea of how I would address it, but with the hope and assumption that the paper would shape itself during its writing and that it would tailor itself to a single theme.

One problem, though: I initially became disinterested in my topic and, although I recognized the fact that I initially had the chance to really hash something out about writing, I realized that I didn't know where to begin, nor what, really, to write about. Nothing jumped out at me until I began to really answer the question "why write?" It took me six pages of essentially stream of consciousness typewriting to realize that what is important to me as a writer is the subject that I am writing about.

If it interests me, if it consumes me, if it virtually writes itself because I am so involved in it, I am happy with the act of writing, but if the topic bores me, if it is a struggle just to complete an assignment, if it isn't any fun to write—then there's nothing in it for me. With this realization, I discarded the dull and tedious previous pages I had written and, in mid-process, began again, if not from the beginning, then from the point my curiosity had been aroused. I was disappointed to find that my first effort turned out to be little more than paper-filling free writing, but then realized that this mid-process change of direction was necessary to achieve some sense of involvement with my own text. Luckily, I still had time to rewrite the paper. Unfortunately, I'm not sure that most student writers will have the inclination or patience to do the same.

I am writing this on a train and find an applicable metaphor in the seat next to mine. It is empty and I hope it will remain so for the duration of the trip. I can lay sideways this way, I can put my feet up, I can spread my stuff out that way. It is very comfortable, and I feel free to do what I want.

For what would I give up this minor luxury?

One, out of necessity, if the train was so full that the empty seat next to mine was the only one available, in which case whoever needed it would sit there and force me to rearrange myself and my gear.

A second scenario arises from the premise in which I can select who I would like to sit next to me. In this case, I would gladly move my bags for someone who I thought I might be interested in talking to, someone who I thought might teach me something. In this scenario, the space next to me is filled because I want to fill it (and with what I want to fill it with), not because it is randomly filled for me in the way it often seems to the student writer that writing topics are assigned.

When I fill the pages with something I am interested in, the trip from beginning to end, from first page to last, goes smoothly and doesn't seem to last as long as the clock and my aching body say it did. Good trips usually come to an end just when we are most consumed by them and when time seems to speed up. A bad writing trip is filled with difficulties and speed bumps, starts and stops, delays, mistakes, misunderstandings and elements of overall badness that conspire to ruin our enjoyment of the scenery. When we get home, we are glad to be back, whereas we don't want the good trip to end.

When we read something we don't like, we put it down and move on to something else, something *good*. Shouldn't it be the same with writers and teachers of writing? If the subject matter is not working, change it in mid-process. Teach the student to not be afraid to change his or her material or their writing process. Inspire them to see that there is subject matter in everything and that they only need to be interested in something to enjoy writing about it more than they would a dull topic, regardless of their skills as writers.

The question, however, becomes somewhat muddled when we apply it to writing students. We say that it is a good thing to assign a topic because it forces the student to complete a piece of work as if it were a model for how that piece of work "should" come out; the instructions come with the box and a grade is given in terms of how close the writer's efforts match or don't match the picture of the "ideal" on the cover of the box. The *assigned* topic, then, provides the writer with a model to complete rather than a project to initiate and execute on one's own terms.

We learn by doing things as we have been taught to do things, but we learn more from attempting to grapple with something new or something in which we feel personally invested. Under this premise of getting the student to write about subject matter that he or she wants to write about, the emphasis should be on getting the student to initiate projects of his or her own rather than on finished products.

This is not to say that there won't be completed papers, but that the completed papers will be a reflection of the student's personality and interests and that they will be works of self-expression more than works of demanded impressions.

AN ORGY OF WRITING

What do you know and what do you need to know? What does it taste like and what can you do with it for lunch? How many times have I asked you not to bother me while I'm writing? What is the point? What do you mean? What are you trying to say?

Do you write for the same reasons that you take pictures? To capture a moment, to create a moment, to remember a moment, to share a moment, to build a personal archive, a private history of things seen, heard, remembered, created, briefly glimpsed? Do you write because you want to re-experience a scene or a moment later or so that someone else who wasn't there can get a sense of the photographed *or* written moment?

Do the same reasons apply to writing? Some, but not all. You write letters to share moments and feelings and to stay in touch with or get to know someone. But why do you write stories? Why do you create fiction? Why do you try to breathe life into something that doesn't exist but that you hope someone will read as if it is real?

You write stories to create worlds and characters and scenes to place them in. You write stories to write stories. You take pictures to take pictures. But why? Just because it feels right?

Write. If it comes naturally, do it, without questions. Just write, but why? Why not? Why do you ask?

Your questions create still more questions until there is nothing left but unanswerable confusion. If you try to explain something that has no answer, something that might not need to be questioned to begin with, will you kill it with your self-conscious thoughts or will random words continue to fall out, in order as well as in full disarray?

What elements combine to form an effective paragraph? Why is writing important? Why should I take my own writing seriously? Why do we have to give and receive grades?

High school typing class: the teacher instructs us to NOT type on the platen. I wonder what will happen if we do. I take the paper out of the machine and discreetly tap out a few lines onto the black cylinder of my taboo platen. Nothing happens. It is fun to type on things you aren't supposed to type on.

Kindergarten vegetable painting: we are supposed to dip carrots and potatoes into trays of paint and stamp the vegetable's design onto pieces of construction paper to make trees and leaves. My friend and I become bored with dipping and stamping. We begin finger painting. When the teacher sees us with our hands in the dish of magenta, we are scolded, told to wash our hands, and leave the painting group to sit facing the wall. A note is given to me at the end of the day to carry home to my parents. After school, I open it and read it. The note politely describes my bad behavior in class that day. I tear it up and throw it in the sewer and when I get home, I have a snack and watch some television. It turns out that my teacher also made a point of calling my mother to tell her that I would be coming home with a note for her. I discover this later at the dinner table when I am asked if I have something to pass along from school. It is my first lesson that there are trap doors and dark alleys and moats and drawbridges, that your first and worst critics are some of your teachers who didn't know the emotional value of platen typing and finger painting.

When Peter invites us to an "orgy of writing," I am initially hesitant and confused. What does he want? How will I be graded for this? What is the assignment? Write. Write what? Write. Just write? Yes. Oh, that's all. Yes, that's all. Fill the pages with reckless abandon.

I wonder how many of us have had teachers who taught similar lessons to us along the way? I remember a few in elementary school, a few in high school, a few in college.

Are just a few in every crowd enough to encourage us to be creative without fear of JUDGMENT?

WHY SHOULD I WRITE?

Why should I bother to sit down and put words on paper? What if I don't want to write? I am not exactly pondering these questions when I wake up on Sunday morning, but they are in the back of the part of my mind where there is a list of things I *should* do to start the week off right. Since Wednesday I have been thinking about what I might like to write as an answer to the questions I came up with, but nothing concrete comes to mind and over the weekend there were many pleasant distractions to choose from: a hurricane to watch pass over, a party to attend, and a daylong road trip to take.

Why should I go sit in the library and write some dreary piece of prose when I have just looked out my bedroom window at a crystal-clear blue sky? Why should I consider one minute of my time as a minute to be spent working on this essay when the air tastes as pure and cold and clear as it looks?

The phone rings. It's my brother. "Road trip," he says and, although I do grab my pen and a small notebook, I put most of my energy into gathering the makings for a hearty lunch to be eaten somewhere beneath the open sky as far from the library as possible.

My Sunday is filled with various forms of peaceful silence and chances for reflection. In retrospect, I don't recall once thinking of my writing assignment at any time of this particular Sunday. My mind was on the road, the music we played, the food we ate, the farms we passed, the woods we passed through, and the expansive views we stopped to look at.

There were four of us in the car and there was a lot of conversation and laughter, but there were also moments of shared silence as if it was understood that this was a to be a day *away* from the world and also a day to be involved with nothing but the world.

I didn't think much about writing except the few times I took out my notebook to jot down the lyrics to a song, the name of a store, a bit of our conversation, and a reminder to use something seen as a scene in a future story:

"Too far gone to turn around..."

"Leonard Eggs..."

"There are no lines on this road, it's just been recently paved."

"A gas station on a quiet Sunday..."

And finally, as my brother and I stared at one of the more awe-inspiring views of the day from the lookout tower above the Quabbin Reservoir, I had what might be one of my most definitive thoughts about writing: YOU CAN'T WRITE LIFE.

This is why, except for those few scribbled notes and a roll of film's worth of pictures taken, the rest of the day was spent without a thought given to writing or the work needing my attention later in the week.

We ate our food at the edge of the Quabbin Reservoir as the sun began to set. The air has cooled considerably. We parked the car above and walked down through two fields separated by a wall of bushes. We walked along the water's edge, looking at the rocks on the ground, listening to the water lap against the shore, looking for the perfect spot to sit and eat. We found a rock to sit on and huddle over our food and shiver as we eat and drink. "I feel like we're Vikings," one of us said. "We may as well be Vikings," someone else said. We're the only ones alive. There's no one else in sight." We ate and talked and laughed and looked at things and there is no way that these small moments could be accurately captured in words. Or could they?

You can try. You can try because there are days that are not so perfectly orchestrated to be lived entirely in a series of perfect moments. There are days when "reality" must be dealt with, when work instead of wonder is required. And there are empty hours that we try to fill with books, movies, artwork, thoughts, and ideas. And some of us fill these hours with writing. I am no closer to an answer as to why I write or why I should write, though. I can make up some answers. I can try to write an essay about it. I can try to convince a future student that writing is important. I can try to write a good story. I can, and will, try all of these things, if only to remind myself of the days in my life that have been spent giving no thought to the demands of the world except to what it has to offer for free when I was able to lose myself in the moment.

I could have described the entire day, the winding roads, the rock formations, the stories and jokes told, etc., but I am stuck between the world and the word and am unable to capture anything except a glimpse of the two separate realms on paper.

How does a writer leave the world behind to create a world of words? How does he or she leave the word behind to make a world out of the world? The writer is outside and inside both. Sunday was an epic day. I will try to write about it someday. Today is Monday. I wonder why it can't still be Sunday.

ME AS A WRITER

Revising bores me. For writing to be exciting, it must pull me in, make me forget the world, and allow me to immerse myself fully in the topic or story at hand.

I wonder where ideas come from as I write. It seems so strange that words can fall out of one's head and on to the blank page. Sometimes when I write, I tune in to the noise of words that is buzzing in my mind and try to watch as one word is chosen over another as it falls through the tube of my pen like one of those winning lottery ping pong balls.

While I write, I feel as if I am being directed towards the correct word or the proper phrase and that the words I choose not to use would have been the wrong ones anyway. When I am fully consumed by a piece of writing and am lost to the din of the process, it feels as if every word is the right word.

I always feel ready to write. If someone told me to sit down and write a story about a man who moves to a desert island to build a golf course, I would be able to sit down and do it in an hour or two.

I can sit down wherever I am and pop off five or six pages without stopping. But whenever I consciously decide to allot some time to writing a given piece that I have had in mind for a long time, it is as if I am suddenly not a writer but simply a person without words.

The stories I write are rarely the ones that I think would make good stories. The ones I write are the ones that almost write themselves. I have pages and pages of story ideas, but I am unable (or unwilling) to sit down and confront them for fear of having no way to start or finish them.

I am a distracted writer these days, in flux with everything. Having moved around so much in the last several years, I have been more tuned in to the importance of developing personal relationships. I don't feel connected to a place without a small group of friends.

Each time I move my writing seems to get put on hold, although I am always taking notes, scribbling lines and broken bits of poems. It is difficult to write when you feel disconnected from your surroundings. I suppose for me this is because I become disconnected from my surroundings when I sit down to write.

I enter an alternate, parallel plane, a realm of when and where that did not and does not exist but suddenly does. It is hard to put down the piece of writing at the end of a session and discover that you don't have anyone to talk to, that there is no human contact waiting at the other end of the writing vacuum in which you have been immersed.

This does not bother me necessarily because I know that after a few months I will have a new group of friends in this new town, but sometimes I stop myself from writing because I know that when I stop writing there will be no slice of "reality" to return to.

On the other hand, I am addicted to change: change of scenery, job, friends, lifestyle. The first months of every move is filled with powerful moments of observation, a heightened sense of awareness, introspection, and self-examination as I wonder what I want to get out of my new surroundings and what is going to happen there.

This has led to growth as a writer for me. It (moving) has accelerated certain perceptions of the craft of writing. Just as I will meet new and interesting people in time and with luck and some effort, so will new stories and styles of storytelling appear.

I have learned to wait patiently for these things. Learning to wait for a routine to develop each time I have moved has allowed me to understand that the same process is applicable to writing: it will come, but you have to work at it, and you have to be patient.

How hard it is to believe one's own advice, though. Revising still bores me. I still become angry when I think I am not doing enough. I urge myself to take writing seriously as if it is the most important thing in the world, but I am constantly distracted from it.

I haven't allowed it to consume me. I haven't let the process of writing fiction have its way with me yet. But still, for no obvious or apparent reason, I continue to write. I think constantly in terms of story and narrative. Despite these ruminations about what I feel I'm doing or not doing, I do write a lot and think about writing all the time.

Me as a writer: I write, but don't know why. I write stories but wonder why I am not out in the world immersed in some real experience instead of seated at this table punching out little words on thin pages.

I wonder what I have to do to let writing come naturally. Instead of waiting for the stories to come, I feel as if I have tried to force them, and by forcing them have driven them away. It is strange to be a writer of fiction, but one of these days I am going to learn to get it right.

Me as a writer: in flux, moving around, curious, confused, awake and aware, exploring, experimental, excited, bored, distracted, unfulfilled, unsatisfied, afraid to draft the definitive draft because I know that in a short amount of time it will feel as if someone else wrote it.

Everything I write feels unfinished. How do I learn to finish a piece, to let it go, to realize its potential? I'm full of questions as a writer (even more so as a person). This is a good sign. There is always something to learn. There is never one right way to write something. There are no rules, only ways, and lots of advice. Who can one believe?

WRITING COMMUNITIES

The interesting thing about a writing community in which an element of trust has been established by the writing instructor is that when you read someone else's work, it is because you are genuinely interested in it.

An effective writing community allows you to share an important aspect of your identity without feeling that you are sharing something too personal. There is great potential in a writing community, but it must be nurtured carefully.

Guidelines for feedback need to be established. The instructor must make an effort to create a feeling, however illusory, of a group effort within the class, and make adjustments as needed to ensure that feedback given and received is extremely constructive.

WRITING

I feel as if my writing is always evolving. I pull out something from a year ago, and it is if someone else had written it. Although I am not necessarily pleased with it because I can see where and how I could have written better or the way I really wanted to write it, the way I think about the writing has been altered by taking time away from it.

I feel more objective about the words I put down on the paper than when I was writing them. I can see more clearly what works and what needs work, and it doesn't feel as painful or frustrating as it did before to not know what I want to write, or how to write it.

With some patience and the usual amount of pain and suffering, the words will come when they want to come. In the meantime, I can free write, seek out feedback, and not worry that I am not getting it right the first time because part of the process is working one's way out of a problem to reach its solution.

I remind myself that there are bigger and more important things than writing. I often have a hard time relating what I write to my life; they are two separate worlds. On the other hand, writing is extremely important to me. We all need something that connects us to life.

I would rather have a successful relationship, though, I would rather connect with another person than with a distant reader.

At the same time, writing is satisfying to me possibly because it fills my mind with the same intensity that a relationship might offer...or at least fills the empty hours that might have been spent with someone with prose and poetry.

Why write? Writing connects readers to life. I can't decide if writing does the same thing for the writer, though. Sometimes I wonder if the writer doesn't know how to live in the world, and so he or she sits inside and writes about it instead.

WILLIAM STAFFORD'S "WRITING"

It is a whisper. You turn somewhere,
hall, street, some great event: the stars
or the lights hold; your next step waits you
and the firm world waits-but
there is a whisper. You always live so,
a being that receives, or partly receives, or
fails to receive each moment's touch.
—William Stafford

In William Stafford's essay "Writing," it seems he is seeking a definition of art and writing. When I read William Stafford's essay, I felt as if I was no closer to possessing a definition of art and of writing, nor that it is entirely practical or possible to define an activity that produces such ambiguous and subjective texts and images. At the same time, I felt as if I was closer to an idea of what art and writing might be and what it has the potential to do: inspire, instruct and enlighten.

By thinking about art and writing, I am at least tuning in to it and its effects on me and my mind, but this does not lead me to try to define it, especially when I see "art" in almost everything: the tied shoelace, the Christmas tree, the manhole cover, the tube of toothpaste, the spacecraft...anything taken a little bit out of its utilitarian context, it seems to me, approaches the silent realm of art, where an object or text exists in and of itself.

Just as museums isolate a specific work of art by giving it its own space, so does the mind isolate things outside of the museum as pieces of art. I don't think that things need to be isolated and put on pedestals to be called art. As Stafford points out, "One doesn't learn how to do art, but one learns that it is possible by a certain adjustment of consciousness to participate in art—it's a natural activity for one not corrupted by mechanical ways."

If art and writing and reading are subjective activities, then it stands to reason that every person will have their own ideas about what they think about when they think about "art." Some don't think about it at all, but those who do may or may not agree with Stafford's views. I would suggest that in any discussion about art and writing, there should be a detour sign placed around "agreement," "understanding," "categorization," and "finalization." No firm conclusions should be drawn. One should recognize that everyone has a different idea about art. Another possibility is that virtually anything that makes a person think, in passing or at length, can be a piece of art, even if it is not a material object, for instance a song or speech.

Anything that affects us in such a way is "art" and anything that affects us and makes us think while doing it is "artistic." We are not promised anything by making art except the possibility of being truly pleased with something that we have created instead of something that someone else created that was then presented to us as an example of "what art is."

The best definition is no definition. The best way to talk about it is to get people to make art and decide for themselves instead of being passive recipients of what the art and writing world says is good. As Stafford points out, "The feel of our lives, instead of being disregarded or slighted, is accepted as important."

In attempting to lay down his ideas about what he thinks art and writing are and what their purpose is, Stafford reveals the essential difficulty that is brought with categorization: he contradicts himself, wittingly or not, not in a spiteful or malicious way, but in a manner that suggests he *knows* that the best he can do is try to make the reader think for him or herself.

In his second point about art, Stafford writes that, "Not a few, but everyone, makes art." Then, in his sixth "tenet," he writes that, "Practical people assume that creating in art takes place in a mechanical manner…No."

If everyone makes art or can make art or thinking artistically, then even "practical" people qualify. This does not mean that they will affect others the same way that "impractical" artists might affect us, whatever the difference between practical and impractical art's effects are, but that there is no right way to classify or define art, its production and creation, and the way we think and talk about it.

It should just be, because the possibility exists that "practical" producers create the practical pieces of art that affect our daily lives: the shoelace, the manhole cover, the tube of toothpaste, the spacecraft; and that "impractical" producers such as Stafford (and hopefully myself, one day), while not creating things that serve utilitarian purposes, continue to find new and enlightening ways to fill the mind with food for thought.

At this point in my life, art and writing are anything that makes us think, but I may be wrong, in fact I am completely wrong because everyone is right. Art may be nothing or it may be everything, depending on who you're talking to.

JANET EMIG'S WEB OF MEANING

It's hard to know what to think of Janet Emig's collection of essays *The Web of Meaning*. Written over a twenty year period, the book represents an academic autobiography in which the reader observes Emig as she works her way into academia as a struggling graduate student looking for her own "paradigms" and "governing gaze," only to turn, in the end, to the full-time writing of poetry or, as Emig says in one of the pre-essay interviews with her editors, "I've stopped talking theory to myself because I want to write and theory informs one's work in one dimension only, but not in another."

When asked, in the same interview, what audience is critically important to her, Emig replies that, "I'm interested in an audience for my poetry. And that's the only one I'm interested in." How, then, is the reader supposed to digest Emig's material if she has implied its meaninglessness to us?

One of the interesting aspects of Emig's book is the fact that it includes, as a preface to each of her essays, a brief interview with the author about the contexts and processes behind each piece. Presented in this manner, the book comes off as an overview of one writer's involvement with the academic community. The reader hears a little bit about what was going on in the author's life at the time of each essay and her thoughts about the essay that follows.

The problem I had while reading Emig's book was that I became more interested in what was implied and hinted at in the pre-essay interviews than the essays themselves. Emig's essays, I thought, never quite seemed to address, in light of what I learned about Emig in the interviews, the issues that she was most interested in, although there are a few pieces that seem to lean in this direction. When one reads that theory informs one's work in only one dimension, one wants to know how and why this is, but Emig says no more about it.

What's strange is that Emig acknowledges her theoretical abilities in the interview before "The Tacit Tradition," when she says, "Initially, what I was able to do was describe; and then after awhile what I was able to do was analyze; and last—and I think it's logical—what I was able to do was theorize."

This statement also serves as an accurate description of the collection in which Emig moves from descriptions of graduate research to analysis and finally to theorizing. In the end, though, her ability to theorize leads her right out of the compositional field. At the point where one theorist might move into some original thinking, Emig discovers that theory, if she lets it, will destroy her *poetic* sensibilities.

Perhaps this is why, after addressing such issues as "The Uses of the Unconscious in Composing," "Children and Metaphor," and "Writing as a Mode of Learning," she concludes her book with a loosely constructed, non-academic piece entitled "Literacy and Freedom."

If there is a central strand that connects Emig's essays to each other, it is her eventual declaration of the fact that, "as teachers and researchers we must try to help make writing natural again, and necessary." In the preface to the first essay in the book, Emig states, "I think that the teaching of writing was deformed in the past as it is in the present by concentrating on what the teacher does, not on what the student writer is experiencing." In "Literacy and Freedom," she declares that "Only by acquiring a public language, literacy, is it possible for us to talk to ourselves and so to acquire a sense of privacy and a true sense of self."

I imagine that, in light of her exit into poetry, Emig sees the academic world, ultimately, as an oppressive force that threatens the writing voices of its students and teachers with blankets of theory. I admired the fact that the author chooses to return to poetry, but in a way, I thought that she was copping out by not composing an essay about that very issue.

What we're left with, then, is a book of academic discourse and theory whose author declares that academic discourse and theory are not able to shed light on one's writing in a multi-dimensional mode; a book that refuses to address this issue except to suggest it; a collection with no center because, in the end, the center does not hold, and Emig opts out for poetry.

These facts are what make *The Web of Meaning* an interesting book to think about, but they are also the facts that prevent the book from being a connected whole because the author neglects to address the most tantalizing ideas that are only suggested in passing.

DISSONANCE & CACOPHONY

DISSONANCE AND CACOPHONY

The Seahawks game tonight was an exercise in dissonance and cacophony. There were glimpses of former forms of precision and glory but the whole thing was a mess. The first punt of the game was botched when the long snapper snapped the ball along the ground through the punter's legs and the Saints dove on the ball and scored a touchdown. A few minutes after, the "cable cam" that hangs on a wire above the field of play malfunctioned and the game was delayed for ten minutes while technicians pulled it away from the action.

The Saints came into this game a hungry and desperate team ready to do anything for a win. They looked sharp and prepared and dominated the Seahawks in every way possible the entire first half. The second half was mostly the same, except that the Seahawks showed signs of life and creativity only to throw it away with more botched plays and botched calls by Coach Holmgren that had John Madden and Al Michaels expressing shock and disbelief at what they were seeing. It was a strange game.

Last year, there were echoes of the Super Bowl team of the year before, but it now seems like each year since the Super Bowl is a watered-down dilution of what the team used to be rather than the rise of a force to be reckoned with in the future.

At halftime, I walked down to Broadway to get some food to go at the Indian place on the corner. I ordered what turned out to be a plain and mostly flavorless chicken and broccoli stir-fry that cost more than the tandoori chicken plate I should have ordered.

There is nothing worse than a botched dinner, but then I was watching a botched game and there was something about the whole Sunday that felt botched from the get-go, having slept poorly all night because of some kind of stomach discomfort that I hoped had more to do with something I ate over the weekend than the stomach flu going around.

Sometimes I wish I was a professional athlete, that my day-to-day satisfaction was based on my day-to-day performance within the confines of whatever team in whatever game I might find myself a part of. But I am not an athlete, and though I have a handful of memorable personal sports moments, my real strength, I hope, lies in the mental games of writing and thinking.

One cannot compete with memory. One can only attempt to create new memories by instigating memorable experiences. Having written that, doesn't the same hold true of writing? Am I not seeking out something memorable in words even though I might simply be continuing a line of thinking on the page that began long ago with other lines on other pages? Isn't the point to create something that feels like an experience?

With this "grasping at the epic" vibe in mind, however, I find that I have to return my thinking to more grounded and mundane matters, as I have just finished grading all but a short stack of the essays that I need to return to my students tomorrow, and now, having used the phrase "short stack" I find myself in the mood for, if not actual pancakes, then at least the idea of pancakes.

In their stead, I have to remind my students to number their pages, properly format their title pages, write a full five pages instead of four and a half pages, that summary is not discussion, that commas are not to be used where they don't belong or left out where they do, that it's best to use a single verb tense throughout, and that the best thing any of them could do to improve their writing would be to slow down, be patient, and explore each and every topic thoughtfully, at the pace of existence, not the pace of the internet, channel surfing, rushing from job to home to job, but having taken the time to find a focus.

I want them to visualize every essay as an experience that exists on the same plane as any other ecstatic experience in their lives, but I cannot instill this idea in them unless they instill it in themselves or have already instilled it in themselves by attempting to live fully and selfishly attracted to capturing their life experiences in words and images on the page.

This is one of the greatest values of writing, its ability to stop and capture time for others to experience later. With this in mind, no one wants to have just a partial experience, and so tonight's Seahawks game leaves a bad taste in the mouth. The game, though, was something to be watched, and really had nothing to do with me, as much as I wanted them to win. My victories and defeats exist on the written page and few people tune in on a nightly basis to see if I am winning or losing.

Why do we seek in things outside of ourselves that which we should be pursuing within? Be it a book or video game or movie or Sunday Night Football, anything we consume is a replacement for something we could have produced ourselves. In the battle between consumption and creation, consumption seems to win most of the time and it's no fault but our own.

A piece of writing should be a conversation with one's reader. The writer should write with their reader in mind and not as if they are talking to themselves. Writers should think of themselves as teachers and ask themselves what they want to teach their readers.

Your readers exist. They pick up your work hoping to be altered and moved in some way. Not only do they hope to find themselves in your words, but they also hope to find a new way of looking at the world.

Picture yourself as a quarterback attempting to get the ball into the end zone where your receivers (readers) wait, hoping for you to find them and connect with both feet inbounds, the crowd going wild.

DEPARTURES & DESTINATIONS

We know what the world is: the world is everything. What, then, does it mean to be "contemporary?" I think we know it when we see it because if it is "contemporary" it is all about what is happening now and almost seems to have arrived from the future, like that feeling when you're standing in a club and a band you're hearing for the first time kicks in with a song that just "makes sense" and you think "yeah" and surrender to the beat.

History, though, isn't so forgiving. In the literary world where critics and thinkers attempt to decide what can be considered "timeless," little thought is given to what makes sense now. The emphasis is placed on what will still make sense years, decades, and centuries from now. If history has proved two things, it is this: one, cycles of repeat themselves and two, one can't predict the future because new advances we could never imagine are always on the horizon.

Before you started to become aware of the world as a thinker and a student of literature, could you have predicted the present state of the world as it is today, immersed in its swirl of scientific and technological advances and their ripple-influencing effects on the arts and media, the emergence of new diseases and gene-altered species, the tempting and dazzling Hubble images from the far reaches of the universe that beckon and invite us out to explore the stars, the consequences of globalization as the world attempts to come to terms with how small it has become as a result of air travel, the internet, e-mail, cell phones and satellite connections, friction between ideologies in the form of religions, economics, nationalities, and cultures, a world threatened with extinction from within and without? What book, what literature, can contain and capture even a portion of everything that is happening?

It's easy to think of literature as the books we read, but isn't it also valid to think of all forms of information, art, and media as part of the literature of the world around us— film, television, internet, advertising, music, art, world events? We will have to decide how we are supposed to proceed in the face of all that is taking place and developing around us as we decide on a course of action for creating our own literary forms and making sense of the world.

STORIES

Stories have played such a central role in my life that it seems almost impossible or implausible to explain their importance in the same way that explaining the importance of my big toe seems like an inherently ridiculous endeavor. How do you explain something so prevalent throughout your life that it seems obvious? My big toe helps me keep my balance. Without it I would be able to walk but my walking would be different, and so my whole life might be different.

Along the same lines, without stories to tell and hear told by others, I would still be alive, but what would that life be like? I can't imagine. "The world is made of language." Terence McKenna has said. This sentiment seemed obvious at first, but when I thought about it further, my indifference to its implications turned into a sense of awe and wonder. What would we be, after all, without language? Still human, yes, but we would simply thrash about in the muck and the underbrush foraging for food with no words to express ourselves. And no stories.

I have always been around people who have told good stories, and in thinking about them now I realize that the reason all these people had good stories to tell is because they had led, and continue to lead, well-lived lives. If you are truly alive, if you are truly open to all of the possibilities that life will throw at you, it is only natural that you will have good stories to tell about your experiences. So, then, the reason that good stories exist in the first place is because the storyteller has experienced something worth telling.

We all have had experiences in bars, at parties, dinners, or wherever a group of friends or strangers have gathered to talk and where good cheer leads to the telling of and exchange of stories. Among every group, there are always those who have more interesting stories than others. We have all experienced the desire to feel like we are part of a group, of some kind of community, of something bigger than ourselves. Often, this desire manifests itself in these storytelling sessions in which people take turns telling their tales and sometimes trying to top or better the last story told.

Depending on the group of people, we have all told or heard a story that fell flat in the telling and was met with a sea of indifference, uncomfortable silence and nervous laughter until the next story began. And we have all had the feeling at one point or another that everyone else in the group had something more interesting or exciting to say than we did or have told a joke and discovered in the middle of its telling that we have forgotten the punch line. The next time around, though, you tell it right, and there is much laughter. So too is it with stories and storytelling.

Your goal should be to first experience things worth telling stories about. Although a trip to the supermarket might inspire some of your most exciting stories—falling in love with someone you see, witnessing some strange or exciting event on your way there or back, running into someone you had lost touch with or hadn't seen in years— more often than not you will simply gather your food, stand on line to pay for it, and head home for dinner. Repeat this routine every day of the year and you might not find yourself with a dazzling array of memories and exciting stories to tell when the new year arrives.

Experiencing new things, meeting new people, deviating from your normal routine, doing something that you had never imagined doing or being able to do until you did it—these are the kinds of things that will create memories worth remembering, and stories worth telling.

I like my friends who have good stories to tell, but they are probably my friends because they are living lives that inspire the telling of good stories and by extension inspire me to travel past the borders of my own internal map of experiences and memories so that I myself might create such epic scenes of beauty for myself to participate in, and remember later in my mind, or on the page in words.

A friend once gave me a story about one of his experiences to read and told me that I probably wouldn't look at him the same way after I read it. In a way, he was right. I did look at him different, but not in the way he might have expected.

I think he expected me to judge him or think of him as a different type of person than whatever he thought I thought before I read his story. The next time I saw him, though, I saw someone who had led an adventurous existence and wasn't afraid to put his stories down on the page in words for others to experience.

Stories can teach us lessons learned by others, and they can teach us about ourselves by helping us make sense of some of the experiences we have had. At their best, though, a good story should inspire us to live an equally adventurous and epic existence and to not just eat at home every night in front of the television.

A good story should make its reader want to head out into the night looking for adventure, or out onto the open road, looking for experience. A good story should inspire us to go out and search for our own good stories.

To be young or old without adventures to look forward to or back on in the movie of the memories in our mind is a curse. Without knowing what comes after we die, we must assume this to be our only life, our only story. With this thought in mind, it should be everyone's goal to make his or her story epic and adventurous and to tell as many people as possible about the incredible scenes of beauty he or she experienced firsthand.

You should have as many stories as possible to tell that are so amazing that no one will believe you when you tell them. You should be able to look back at the things you have done and the things that have happened to you with a measure of disbelief.

And when you are involved in these epic stories of your life, when they are happening and you can't believe your good fortune, make sure to step outside yourself for just a moment to remind yourself that, "this will make a good story someday."

"THE WORLD IS MADE OF LANGUAGE."
--TERENCE MCKENNA

Think about the above statement for a moment. I mean, *really* think about it. It seems simple at first and even a bit obvious: the world is made of the words we use to make the world.

Now think of the profound impact of the statement. If reality is shaped by the words we use to create it, then why doesn't the world more resemble what we'd like it to be?

Could it be that at any given time there is a struggle between competing "vocal aggressors" all vying to shape the world in the language that most resembles their desires?

Think about the above statement again. Think about its implications. How is language used by your family, your friends, the media? How is language used in your everyday relationships? How are you using language? To what end?

Ideas spread through language. William Burroughs wrote, "language is a virus." So, then, the words you say and the words you write are never *just* words, there is a greater dynamic at work, a greater struggle that is taking place at any given time.

You want to be heard, but it is just as important, maybe even more important to listen. When you listen, when you really listen to the ways in which language is used, you will see some patterns. You might notice that language is used to enforce and enable power structures and authority. You might notice that language is used to manipulate behavior. Just listen to what is being said throughout the course of one of your days. Listen to how it is being said and think about what effect it is supposed to have.

On the brighter side of things, you might notice that language is also used to educate and enlighten, and in the best scheme of things possible, you might hear language being used in a purely visionary form.

When you step outside your normal everyday use of language to write as a poet, you become a visionary. When you use language to express things that aren't easy to express in words, you become a visionary. When you put into words something no one has been able to express but that they had been subconsciously thinking, you become a visionary.

Members of earlier civilizations set out from their villages in search of new land, property, fortune, discovery. At some point, these early explorers returned to their villages and with whatever goods they brought back with them they also brought stories. These stories probably inspired others to set out on their own journeys to see what was out there.

If writing is about capturing experiences, and capturing experiences is all about exploring the world in search of those experiences, then at the heart of all writing is a spirit of exploration.

We should have no limits to the boundaries we are willing to at least attempt. I am drawn to art and literature that pushes the boundaries of the known, that stretches the edge of what seems familiar, and that inspires others to set out on their own boundary explorations and come back with their own stories to tell, their own art and literature.

We might not be able to leave the planet (yet), and we might not be satisfied with everyday reality, but if you are a visionary writer or exploring the language or ideas of being a visionary in your work, you know that your goal is to push the boundaries further.

Yes, what is new is only new for a while and then becomes assimilated into mainstream culture, but there's nothing wrong with that, it's all part of the process of constantly moving forward and evolving.

Before you dive into your work, ponder the magnitude of the literary and artistic heritage that has gone before you and that whatever your tastes are, you have allies in the past, and therefore, by extension, the present and future who you will be expressing yourself to. You are part of this continuum or, as Gary Snyder refers to it, "…the Great Subculture which runs underground all through history…" You have all the tools necessary to be a visionary. How are you going to use your language to shape/reshape the world?

POEM

A poem, if it is not the experience itself, is the diluted spirit of the experience. This is enough for experience, but not for poetry.

We must seek the extreme in life and in art. Extreme experiences raise our level of awareness. By introducing elements of the impossible into our lives, or at least what we were once unable to imagine becoming real, the impossible becomes possible, the unreal becomes real and forward progress is made.

Science and art raise the level of awareness and reality by introducing new realities to the world. Our minds must be ready for them. We have entered a new age of technology and technicians. We are in the midst of raising our levels of awareness on a grand and epic scale.

We must prepare ourselves to fight deathray with liferay. We must prepare ourselves to fight confusion and lethargy with clarity of purpose and conscious acts with tangible, realizable effects. Art and writing are the weapons of choice.

We are entering a time of great change and revolution. Those who can see through to the new reality we are about to enter will seek the edges of the universe for new truths and the answers that lie in wait for us beyond.

A great age of chaos approaches. It is the chaos of reinvention and creativity, a new universal order of thought, language, image, sound, science, and technology. Poetry should reflect this.

WRITERS, ARTISTS, TAIKONAUTS

It's pretty cool that China just put their first man in space and that they have declared ambitious plans to be a force in the future exploration of outer space. It's fairly pathetic how indifferent people have allowed their imaginations to become about space travel. Is it because they have seen too many movies about space travel and are unable to conceive that what is really out there is beyond the conception of any of Hollywood's depictions of the infinite realm?

I possess my own cynicisms, but still seem to find the same sense of wonder I had when I was a kid about space, space travel, and the mystery of what is out there beyond what our current level of scientific ability is able to comprehend.

Our leaders need to make a greater effort to capture the world's imagination.

Here on Planet Earth, we've just finished the third week of classes. The writing is developing nicely. My students might not see it in their work yet, but I do. I can help them become strong writers, but I can't force them to become more enthusiastic about the actual writing process.

When I think of the word writing, I think of it more as a verb than a noun. Verbs are all about action and writing, and though it might appear to be a quiet and slow form of action, writing has at its root the ability to alter thoughts and consciousness, and therefore reality.

Sometimes it helps to think of writing as not just something done on the page. In a worst-case scenario, we live parts of our lives on autopilot as if our scenes are being written for us. In a best-case scenario, when we figure out what we want to do and think up a plan to achieve those ends, we become the scriptwriters of our own lives.

I like to think that some of the topics, films, ideas, and writers we look at in my writing classes understand the connection between writing and living. That's just one possible connection to be made from the material, though.

There's also the pure and simple power of individual storytelling and essay writing and deciding how you want to tell that story or convey the information you want your essay to convey.

What do you want to teach your reader? How do you want to alter the reader's reality in some small or large way? These are just a few of the questions I try to get my students to think about as writers. As thinkers, I give them another set of questions to ponder. Are there connections to be made between the different materials we're looking at? Do you see any patterns developing? Are there any missing links you feel you need to bring to the table? What is going on? Does anyone have any answers yet? We need to be writing the answers.

RULES TO GUIDE YOU

I've often said, "No writer should ever allow another writer to tell them how to write." As an act of creativity, writing is a private art form in which each writer creates their own rules to follow as they attempt to put into words whatever it is they are trying to express.

Being a writing teacher carries with it its own form of conflict with the above. If I believe that no writer should tell another writer how to write, how do writers come to terms with being a teacher of classes in which students are looking for guidance or simply trying to figure out what they need to do to get a good?

The key word in the above paragraph is guidance. The teacher should act as a guide and not a dictator of taste, style, and previously explored writing "rules." A guide points things out to you along the way and shows you things they think are worthy of note. A good guide won't tell you what you should think about those things. A good guide will provide you, perhaps, with some context to get your thoughts flowing and then let you work through the experience on your own.

"On your own." This is a key phrase that is essential to the writing and creative processes because as much as a writing teacher can guide a student writer and encourage them to "look at the sights," it is the writer's responsibility to figure out what to make of the places visited and define for themselves the form their writing about those places will take.

A good teacher/guide attempts to stay out of the way of the creative process as much as possible and, as much as possible, encourage independent thought.

ABOUT POETRY

Write poems, however they appear, whenever they appear, whatever they look like, however they sound, and whatever they're about. Form belongs to function. You are not writing a chair. Poetry is not really the "craft" that some poets think it is. Building a chair is a craft. All poetry can be stretched out into a straight single line the same way a chair made from metal could be stretched and spun into wire.

This wire would not be the best way to present a "chair" to someone who needed to sit down, but were one to stream every line one had ever written in a single straight line such as on the news scroll at Times Square in New York City, the poem or poems or single long poem that one is really working on from the first word one writes until the last would still exist for the reader standing on the street below. Your time would be better spent writing a poem (having an experience) than dissecting the act of writing a poem.

Only a carpenter looks at another carpenter's work and thinks about how they could make a better chair. Only poets look at other poets' poems and think about how they could write a better poem. Your poems don't belong to you, really, they belong to your readers. I hope this helps.

ON BOOKSTORES

I feel safe and at home in bookstores. I know where I'm at. I know what to do. Things become clear. I am no longer wandering down the street enjoying a lazy afternoon, I am wandering through "the life of the mind" (*Barton Fink*).

While there are statistics that say Seattle is a big reading town, I don't think there are nearly enough bookstores compared to other cities I have either visited or lived. Until recently, there were four in my neighborhood, enough to keep me occupied and happy to at least have a few nearby options, though three of them have since closed, leaving me with just one bookstore and a couple thrift shops to serve my used book needs.

In a more "urban" city such as Boston or New York, walking between bookstores is part of the joy of bookstore browsing and used book hunting. What's "in between" bookstores in Seattle is not all that interesting. Yes, there are nice trees and houses, but no sense of the "hustle and bustle" of grittier cities, where bookstores become even more crucial to one's survival by offering sanctuary to all who seek them out.

At Book Soup on Sunset in Hollywood across from Tower Records, Sean Penn called me "dude" when we were talking about Charles Bukowski. I was there for the book signing of Dennis Hopper's book of black and white photos. Hopper was seated behind a table, signing books, and laughing a lot with those who approached him, and I found myself standing next to Sean Penn. This was when he was married to Madonna. He had written and published some poems in a few small Los Angeles literary magazines I had read. I don't remember exactly how we started talking, though I knew he was friends with Bukowski at the time. He and Madonna had dinner with Bukowski quite frequently, I had read.

Penn suggested I read *War All the Time*, a collection I hadn't yet gotten to, and specifically a poem called "Good Time Girl." "Read 'Good Time Girl,' dude," he said, and handed me the book. As I read the poem, I thought to myself, "Sean Penn just called me *dude*." Dennis Hopper laughed in the background. Epic.

While browsing at another Los Angeles bookstore I watched as actor Jeff Bridges did his last-minute Christmas shopping. He moved quickly around the store, picking large expensive photo books from the shelves and stacking them near the register. Pretty soon he had two stacks of books almost three feet high, pulled out a credit card and asked if he could get some help getting the books into his car.

David Mamet, the playwright, screenwriter, and director was a regular customer at the bookstore I worked in Cambridge, Massachusetts. I had just returned in April from a year living in Belgium and was going to start grad school at UMass, Amherst in the fall. I took a cab into Cambridge with two hundred dollars in my pocket, thirty of which went to my hotel room that first night back in the United States.

I needed a job bad and had absolutely no plan for how I was going to make ends meet and find a place to live. Looking back on this period now, I realize how precarious my situation was, but I was younger then and unaware of the existence of my shaky perch even though I was standing right on it.

Walking around Cambridge that first day I saw a bookstore that was in the end phase of construction. The doors were open, and people were inside setting up shelves and cash registers. There was a lot of hammering and yelling going on. I asked if they were hiring. I always wanted to work in a bookstore and thought it would be an idyllic job.

The boss was a man with a face just like the one in Munch's painting "The Scream." I filled out an application while talking about my year in Europe to a nice woman I soon became friends with who loved European literature and had recently been to Paris. The boss looked at my application sitting on the stairs leading from one level of the store to the next, looked up at me, held out his hand and said, "You're in." I started the next day.

Those first two weeks we worked sixty or seventy hours a week to get the store set up, the books in place, and everything ready to go. Working in a bookstore was not the peaceful job I thought it would be, though. I thought there would be free time to read, but the boss wanted us to always be doing something, and if there wasn't anything to do, we needed to pretend to do something, which usually meant standing with a feather duster in hand at all times the boss was in the store so that when he came to your area you could transition from staring into space to dusting the same books you had already dusted several times during your shift.

It was a good job, though, and paid for my stay in a boarding house for a month and a half until I had enough money to move into a room in a house not far from the bookstore. Just like that, I was living in Boston.

I have some fond memories of Cambridge, specifically hanging out with my bookstore friends after work and wandering alone on weekends from used bookstore to used bookstore. Cambridge at that time was bookstore paradise. I discovered many authors that summer who are still dear to me to this day and arrived for grad school knowing about a lot of writers few of my fellow grad students had heard of, just from book shopping in Cambridge.

Daily life in the bookstore was not unpleasant, just a little tense because of our manic boss. I gained his trust, though, and he made me the Sunday manager, which meant I opened the store early in the morning and ran it until dinnertime when the Sunday night manager came in. Most Sundays, we started off at the store's espresso stand, where we made outrageously strong concoctions that were not on the menu. All of us hopped up on caffeine, we'd select some CD from the CD collection that the boss would never play. I was partial to playing Christmas music, even though it was summer. I've always liked Christmas music in the summer.

One Sunday, the boss showed up unannounced, heard the music playing, made us shut it off, and asked me to never play it again until the holidays. I agreed, but a few Sundays after, I could not resist. The staff got a laugh out of it, so why not?

That Sunday, a customer said, while buying a book, "Christmas music in August. Unbelievable. It just gets earlier and earlier." On his way out, I politely said, "Happy Holidays." He stopped at the door, turned, looked at me, laughed a little and shook his head. The next few weeks were a blur of activity for me as I traveled back and forth between Boston and Amherst to try to find a place to live and get things set up at school.

Finally, the end of summer arrived, and I had one more day of work at the bookstore. The night before, my boss implied that he was going to throw a going away party for me, so when I woke up the next morning, I was both looking forward to my last day of work and was also sad that my time there was coming to an end.

I had made some good friends, but it was time to move on and begin grad school. Looking back on it, that bookstore probably saved my life and maybe even kept me from being homeless. What if I hadn't found that job my first day back in the United States? How long would my two hundred dollars have lasted? The phone rang early my last morning. It was my boss, and he was angry.

"I thought I told you to never play that goddamn Christmas music again," he growled. Still half asleep, I muttered, "Uh, what are you talking about?" He then read me a letter written by the customer I had wished "Happy Holidays" to almost a month earlier. The writer described me and the other clerk as being very rude to him. This was strange, because he was laughing about the Christmas music while paying for his books but now described my sincere "Happy Holidays" as a personal insult. The letter was inaccurate, but still, this man had gone home and weeks later decided to sit down and write a letter about it to the bookstore owner, who then said to me, "I never want to see your face in my store again."

After hanging up the phone, I was simultaneously upset and laughing at the absurdity of the whole thing. I was upset because now I wasn't sure how I'd see my bookstore friends one last time (we ended up arranging to meet for beers later that night) and because I felt like I'd let the boss down. I was laughing because I had gotten fired from my bookstore job on the last day of work for playing Christmas music in August. Epic.

The bookstore is no longer there. It went out of business five years after I helped open it. I would have liked to have shared a toast with the boss that last day and thanked him for the opportunity. Wherever you are, man, cheers and thank you.

Once I was set up in my new house in Amherst, I wandered around the main strip, found that this very small town had a nice selection of used bookstores, and immediately began adding to the modest collection I had gathered in Boston.

A seven-mile bus ride to Northampton revealed a couple better used bookstores, so I felt right at home and immediately started a routine of going into town every Saturday for the book shopping rounds and Chinese food for lunch. In both Cambridge and Amherst, every new city I've moved to, actually, bookstores have acted as welcome sanctuaries before I knew anyone and had made any friends. Books and bookstores are always there for you even when people are not.

Once I started grad school and met other writers who were book aficionados, book shopping reached a whole new level. Shopping alone is one thing; shopping with a fellow book enthusiast is another and, depending on the friend, is either a competitive safari or a collaborative endeavor.

Sometimes you find yourself feeling jealous about what the other person found or happy that you were the one to find it first. Sometimes you're with a friend who finds a good score but knows it's a book that belongs on your shelf more than theirs and hands it over to you (you need to do the same in kind the next time it happens in reverse). Better yet is when you're on a book safari and there are multiple copies of rare or hard to find books by obscure authors so everyone who wants one gets a copy.

The best book safari I went on was with my grad school friend and poet Frank Johnson when we took the bus down to Boston and stayed at his friend's apartment in the heart of Cambridge. Frank and I got up early the day after we arrived, intent on a full day of book shopping. We had a lot of territory to cover. We each spent close to three hundred dollars on books that day, at the end of which we both had heavy double paper grocery shopping bags in each hand and sore feet and arms. That was a good day.

I miss the old days of my former used bookstore cities, but you have to make do with what is around you. There are bookstores in downtown Seattle and bookstores in the U-District, so it's not like we're wanting here, it's just that there isn't the same density of concentration like there was in Cambridge and Amherst, though things have probably changed there too with all the independent bookstores going out of business because of the big chains and the arrival of online shopping.

My friends Sean and Amy used to run Pistil Books in the space that is now the Cha Cha Lounge on Pike. It was a great store and a great place to duck into when it was raining. A month or two before they closed the store to start their online bookselling business, my band played in the store window with lit candles rigged to our winter caps. I think more bands should play in bookstores. Customers browsed and read as we played. I felt right at home.

LOVE & BOOKS IN THE U-DISTRICT

I pulled the cord to get off the #43 bus just after The Henry, walked towards the Magus bookstore, and felt immediately better now that I was on the bookstore corridor.

I crossed over to University Used and Rare and stepped into its well-lit classical music-filled leisure couch-reading environment while the elegant older gentleman/store owner behind the counter priced books as kittens battled each other at his feet (note: this store no longer exists).

I enjoyed being caught in the nowhere time between 2 and 4 p.m. when there's a breathless feeling in the air that seems conducive to falling in love.

We may think we go to bookstores for books, but don't we really go to run into someone holding a volume of one of our favorite authors?

Does that only happen in movies set in other cities? And why do bands in this town not elect to play more often inside our bookstores?

The UW bookstore was next. I reveled in their discount remainder section; they always have something worth taking home.

A few minutes later, I discovered the new Newberry Books below The Grand Illusion; too early in the day for a movie for me, but I imagined the pure joy of waiting to see a movie and being tempted to miss it by some discovered volume found below.

I wandered a bit further up into that lonely bit of the Ave. that feels like a street in a Southern California beach town and discovered an interesting but closed used bookstore and bindery/print shop.

Now totally weak with hunger and filled with unmet love, I proceeded with a sense of joy towards the mecca of Seattle bookstores: Half Price Books.

I book-dreamed through poetry, fiction, literary criticism, and oversize art books until I could no longer take it and had to step next door to Trader Joe's for a lunch of free ravioli samples.

On a good day, I would continue down 45th to The Poem Emporium, a wonderful store filled with poetry that deserves a much more central location (nearer my apartment) to be fully appreciated by the entire city.

If you don't find love or if you only find the potential of love in the eyes of strangers and end up back on the bus heading home, take comfort in the fact that in your bag, for under ten dollars, you found a half dozen titles to carry you through the night.

Get dressed up and go fall in love.

"POST-LITERATE" CULTURE, A RESPONSE

I don't disagree with Charles Johnson's idea that people are less literary and less well-read than they may have been in the past, nor do I disagree that illiteracy is a problem, and as a teacher I obviously agree that education and a well-rounded base of knowledge are important. The problem I have with Charles Johnson's April 2007 column in the *Seattle P-I* has to do with the support arguments and examples he chooses to illustrate his ideas. His introduction and conclusion are effective, but if the introduction and conclusion are the bread of an essay sandwich, then my brain's stomach is left feeling hungry from the absence of "meat" between them.

Johnson blames numerous forms of media for causing society to enter a phase of "post-literacy." Before I decided how to respond to this, I had to think about the new media that has arrived to replace reading, because if people reading, then they must be doing other things. If those other things are YouTube clips, graphic novels, MySpace and Facebook pages, blogs, cell phone movies, downloading, surfing the web, playing video games (Immersive Virtual Novels?), then don't these qualify as gauges of a new and EVOLVING state of culture rather than its demise? And if one of the definitions of the verb "to read" is "to make out the significance of by scrutiny or observation," then isn't there a whole lot of "reading" going on (albeit in new forms) that represents a possible New Literacy? Johnson doesn't seem to think so.

Johnson cites a 2004 N.E.A. assessment of reading habits that found "for the first time in our history, less than half the adult population reads fiction, poetry, or plays." This fact is disheartening, especially for me as a writer, but Johnson then cites former N.Y. Times Book Review editor Charles McGrath, who says that "the really scary news…" [of the study is that] "while the number of people reading literature has gone down, the number of people trying to write it has gone up. We seem to be slowly turning into a nation of 'creative writers,' more interested in what we have to say ourselves than in reading or thinking about what anyone else has to say." If more people are writing and therefore being creative and expressing themselves, isn't this a good thing? Johnson doesn't seem to think so.

While teachers teach, their students are also teaching them about the world, and if there is anything one should know from these exchanges, it is that culture is always in flux. If you are going to reject something outright, then you should replace it with something of your own design. So, I agree with Johnson in that if you see an ill in the world, whether it be artistic or political, you ought to present your vision of reality in the work you create. Johnson's essay does just this. Be careful, though, of insulting the tastes of others, especially if you haven't fully thought through the potential of these things to shape the future of what we perceive to be reality.

Video games, for instance, are a form of storytelling. "What's the difference between a novel and a video game?"

a student might ask. "Aren't they the same?" As for the comic books, manga, anime, and graphic novels that Johnson assails in his piece, Europe and Asia have been way ahead of us in accepting these art forms as more than childhood obsessions for a long time.

Among his many ideas considered too "out there" for serious academic consideration, the late psychonaut Terence McKenna had a theory that we are witnessing the death of print as the primary form of communication and are moving instead into a visual-virtual age that will see us evolve into using a language of projected visual holographs.

He was speaking about a form of telepathy, but perhaps his idea works better as an analogy for memes, codes, and referentiality. If, as McKenna stated, "the world is made of language," then everything we say helps to create the world around us and all forms of art, highbrow or lowbrow, are part of that language that makes up the building blocks of the myths and metaphors of our times.

There's an episode of Star Trek: The Next Generation in which Captain Picard finds himself alone on a hostile planet with an alien who speaks only in metaphors relevant to the mythology of its culture. Picard must decipher these metaphors to prevent hostilities from breaking out between their two cultures. The moment of revelation arrives when Picard exclaims, "you're using METAPHOR!"

In the end he relays his understanding of these metaphors to the other aliens in their spaceship above the planet awaiting news of the outcome of the interaction below. Hostilities are averted; understanding is achieved. Shouldn't we be building such metaphorical bridges too?

Is it really a bad thing that some metaphors of common language are visual in nature? No. The bad thing is that the writers and creators of these media haven't fully taken advantage of the notion of injecting intelligent visual metaphors into their creations…or have they? Courses on The Simpsons are taught at many American college campuses as a form of cultural study and as noted by Dr. Daudi Abe, courses on Hip Hop are blooming in both college and high school classrooms.

I don't want to become one of those adults who rail grouchily about the way things were and then try to assign blame for why things have changed. These are the new "good old days" and whether one is just beginning their education or is an esteemed university professor, it should be clear to see that we are witnessing an explosion of possibility, technology, and creativity that historians will one day look back on as a decisive period of revolutionary change the world over.

Like it or not, we're heading towards a fully immersive virtual reality art culture whose participants and creators won't differentiate between "real" and "fake" the same way we make those distinctions now. Welcome to the New Real.

When I was a kid, we played the Coleco handheld football game during lunch break. A few years later it was Atari and Intellivision, *Asteroids* and *Defender*. Compared to the sophisticated imagery of video games and visual culture today, these examples are nothing more than primitive light blips, so it's no wonder all the new visual possibilities capture our attention. In the words of U2, it's "even better than the real thing."

People in every generation have their own forms of inspiration, their own visual, written, musical, and spoken languages in addition to the technology and media of the time used to create and present the ideas and images that will one day define that age.

The point of living in epic times is to retain one's sense of wonder, or at lease curiosity and engagement. Artist Tabetha Warren offers an appropriate prescription for malaise when she writes, "the person of the future faces a new challenge, to balance the organic with the inorganic, to maintain that spark some call the soul, to be drunk on the wine of the old world while standing on the shores of the new."

We should be open to as much as we can assimilate because if we reject what is new or can't at least attempt to understand what is happening, then we run the risk of rejecting the future itself. The future is where it's at.

OLD LIONS

What happens to old lions? I went out into the night to find out, and this is what I wrote:

Dear Mr. Plimpton, this is both a bill and a thank you note for a night that got me out of the house; got me both nothing and more than I expected; got me to acknowledge that life in all its strange glory is truly unexpected and therefore glorious.

I would not like anything I wrote to be construed as criticism in the purely destructive sense of the word, nor would I want it to be seen as purely derogatory in an outsider looking in kind of way, which begs my first question: why do I always seek the thrill of sneaking my way into the places I know I belong?

Tonight began a week ago when our local events paper made mention of your lecture at Benaroya Hall. I went to see Ann Charters with a friend last week and was thoroughly invigorated with the lecture vibe I had long ago sworn off as nothing but a bunch of talk.

Damn, Mr. Plimpton, now that I am home, I realize that I really enjoyed your lecture, but did I enjoy it for what you said, for what I felt like I paid to hear you say, or for what I accidentally ended up hearing? Or, because you were speaking about writers and writing (sort of), did I learn exactly what I needed to learn?

I guess I would like to leave it as a multiple-choice question and let the reader decide which answer is most appropriate, because I will promise this, Mr. Plimpton and the reading public: I will never allow such an exorbitant fee to be charged in my name and any words I might share with the reading public as you did, sir.

I would like to comment on your lecture first and then proceed with my own gleanings of what the night was "supposed" to teach. I bought my ticket at five-thirty.

"The pre-lecture has just begun," my ticket seller told me. I thanked her out loud, thought about the time, and wondered to myself, "pre-lecture?" You were scheduled to go on two hours later. Was there really two hours of your work to discuss or did I miss out on you yourself emerging from the wings to discuss or read some manuscript of wonderful obscuras that you had stacked away for no one to read but the Pre-Lecture Set?

I was hungry. In fact, I was starving and had my mind set on the Alibi Room, so, with my student ticket conveniently tucked into my front pocket, I now bent a bit forward into the rain and wind with the intention of feeding my shaky soul and possibly running into another soul.

I took my seat at the bar. Evidence of the bartender's half-eaten shift meal of salmon rested on a plate behind the bar. It was exactly what I wanted. I ordered a glass of house white Sardinian at the bartender's suggestion. It was, as he put it, "really, really nice." The salmon was also perfect. The first bite melted in my mouth. The garlic mashed potatoes gave me a wonderfully needed flush of warmth. The bok choy was splendid in its garlicky presentation.

There was an indescribable butter slash hot red pepper slash sugar concoction on top of the salmon; I used it liberally with bites of both fish and potato and liked the way it felt on my tongue. Around the side of the plate was something that looked like drizzled hot fudge; I conjectured briefly with a bit of horror that perhaps I had been served a dessert plate, but when I ran my fork through it and let the sauce dance on my tongue, it turned out to be a balsamic reduction that illuminated every flavor I tasted after.

After I paid my bill, I swayed a bit through the drizzly night. Mr. Plimpton, even though it is not in line with the narrative of my story, I want to say now that your cheap shot about the weather was totally misbegotten. You mentioned that you were surprised to see so many people come out for your lecture with this weather in mind, and then you said something along the lines that you had heard that on nights like tonight in Seattle, there was really "nothing to do."

What you did not realize because you do not live here and because you experience your own type of weather patterns where you do live is that this is the most wild and alive time to be in Seattle each year and that the people in your audience were all expressing their distinct rebellion against such rain in addition to their own desire to be satiated with equally rebellious ideas.

Mr. Plimpton, you made the mistake of trying to play to the hometown crowd who were so very much on your side right from the start. Advice to future famous writers and editors who find themselves accidentally or intentionally fortunate enough to address symphony halls on Tuesday nights about literary matters: don't play to the hometown crowd. Ask them what life is like where they live and listen to their answers, but don't pretend to know things you don't and that aren't even true.

I found a wonderful seat at the back of the first balcony. I would call it "The President's Seat" for if he (or she) were in town for an event, it is exactly where they would be seated: a perfect though faraway view of the stage combined with a perfect though faraway view of the entire audience.

The Black Russian I ordered for $7.25 in the lobby, on the other hand, was anything BUT "presidential." The liquid in the glass barely tapped the halfway point. I looked the bartender in his eyes and realized that he was not really a bartender but just a pourer of the liquids that just happened to be arranged in front of him. I did not complain but asked that he top my beverage off with a splash of soda.

I drank my drink, looked around the lobby, took my seat, exchanged some idle banter and pleasantries with the woman seated next to me, and waited to hear what was going to be said when the lights dimmed. You announced to the crowd that you were going to cover two topics: your experiences with "participatory journalism" and the interviews with authors you published in *The Paris Review*.

The crowd seemed to laugh easily at almost everything you said. I wondered for a minute if perhaps I was in a down or existential mood because I did not find anything you said remotely funny. You went on to review stories I had already heard in anecdotal form, then went on to recount, or rather, re-*read* quotes from authors you had interviewed over the years in *The Paris Review* which, to your punk rock credit, Mr. Plimpton, the title was explained to be in the spirit of youthful dissent both an imitation of *The Partisan Review* and hopefully construed by most readers as a *revue* rather than a *Review*.

Either way, Mr. Plimpton, you created some literary history that any youthful literary magazine editor in whatever media, print or electronic, would do best to subjugate and overthrow with their own ideas of future literary history out of respect for your accomplishments.

I was left to wonder if I paid to hear you recount quotes from other authors about writing from the past rather than the present or future. I was left to ponder how much you were going to be paid for the evening's transaction. I was left to wonder why I had come out knowing I should have stayed home to write even though I knew that I needed to go out into the night to find out the answer to that question.

Was it to sit amongst people much more settled in reality than myself to understand the reader's mind, because I did ask one woman who asked, thinking I had a notebook in my hand instead of a real book, whether I had taken any "good notes," if the lecture had inspired her to write, to which she laughed and said "No, it inspired me to read," to which I

74

laughed and judged her poorly in that moment by thinking that writing was all that one would go to a lecture to be inspired to do.

Now that I am home, though, I too am inspired to read even though I had already read everything you made mention of; even though the only books I really responded to you mentioning were Hemingway's *A Moveable Feast* and the writing of Gertrude Stein. Most of your selections were fairly conservative literary choices and I did not hear you utter one word about any writers currently writing today.

Only three questions were allowed from the audience, the last of which had to do with who you thought was going to win the Super Bowl. You were correct in your prediction or hope that the Oakland Raiders were going to win. I was surprised to hear the crowd I had thought to be so literary hiss in favor of the Tampa Bay Buccaneers. Why would this weird town root for anything but the underdog, I wondered, and why had they not hissed earlier in the lecture?

Suddenly the lecture was over, and your dramatic shock of white hair ambled off the stage. As I left my balcony perch, I noticed appetizers and wine being set up for the Patron's Reception. I had a red ticket; one needed a blue ticket to get in. The author was expected. A posted sign read, "No autographs."

I tried to picture a fanatic George Plimpton reader with all your books in hand, hoping nervously for an autograph. I figured the night was ending, so I walked downstairs to the lobby.

As I walked towards the door, I saw someone's blue V.I.P. ticket on the ground and picked it up. I was now a Patron and mounted the very stairs I had just descended.

After a free glass of chardonnay and two short discussions with women who had been sitting in my section and approached me with the very same question previously mentioned ("did you take any good notes?), I found myself within earshot as you made your way through the crowd, Mr. Plimpton.

The two women I talked to had somehow managed to distract me from the idea of giving you one of my own books which contained, among other published works, a couple poems that your own magazine had seen fit to reject. For a budding or even partially experienced writer, *The Paris Review* is still a lofty goal that one wishes to attain.

I was left to wonder, though, about the legitimacy of a magazine that one person (you) started now being in the editorial and reading hands of other people. No matter how many thousands of manuscripts you must receive, Mr. Plimpton, your magazine simply does not exist unless you are the only one reading everything that comes across your desk.

The aforementioned audience members I chatted with kept me from any possibly awkward encounter I might have had with the literary lion you are. Upon leaving, I tore out the page from my book I had inscribed to "Mr. P.," tore it up, and threw it through the rainy air into a decrepit bus stop garbage can.

You disappeared into the luxurious caverns of the symphony hall and towards whatever manicured wonderful hotel suite the lecture organizers had procured for you. Was it nights like these that I aspired to as a writer myself? I do not know.

I walked home in the rain, fifty dollars poorer but infinitely richer for the knowledge I realized I already knew. Still, Mr. Plimpton, you are a strange literary angel and an old lion who managed to coax other old lions and lionesses out into the night. For that, you and your literary vitality should be commended.

As I ambled off into the rainy night, I imagined what would have been a perfect exchange, and had I been able to say it in the proper tone so that you might pick up its simultaneous ironic intention and laconic truth, I would have said with a slight smirk and one raised eyebrow, "Hello, Mr. Plimpton, here's my book. I'm a faker too."

BE A VISIONARY

What do we understand? What do we need to understand? Is it even important to understand, to make connections, or is it simply important to be able to witness and recognize what is happening until we find our place in the bigger scheme of things?

Everything is changing rapidly now, but life is fundamentally the same: we need to pay the bills, fill our stomachs with food, and rent warm shelter to get us through the night. I like to think that we will embrace some kind of visionary, forward-thinking reality, but I don't expect human nature to change, and we will always need to fulfill these basic human needs.

Various writers and thinkers are visionary in their own way. The Russian Futurist Velimir Khlebnikov, around the time of the revolution in 1917, wrote about radio and movie messages in the sky and the creation of a universal language that would be understood by all. Today, Brian Eno pushes forward with his ongoing evolution towards the creation of future music, media, and creative applications of technology.

Terence McKenna, dead too soon and unable to continue playing the role of cultural techno-shaman, points us towards the "eschaton," some kind of event that will radically alter our reality. It remains to be seen if this event is, as he has suggested, anything ranging from the arrival of flying saucers to an earth-threatening natural disaster to some kind of life-altering computer program, but we can easily see that at the rate our technologies are developing very interesting times are ahead.

Despite all the above, existence is still about the individual finding his or her way through life. The narrator of Emmanuel Bove's novel *My Friends* is an odd, lonely soul wandering Paris without a job as he yearns for one true friend.

Paul Leppin's Severin in *Severin's Journey into The Dark* and Harry Joy in Peter Carey's *Bliss* are individuals who sense a greater reality just out of reach. Severin's is a soul filled with unrest and discord. He steps dangerously close to the edge of self-destruction in his search for experience and after the final chapter of this strangely beautiful book, one would be hard-pressed to guess whether he finds his way back into the circle of humanity.

Without Honey Barbara appearing in *Bliss*, Harry Joy might have remained lost and disillusioned, but she leads him to a natural and organic state of being more in harmony with nature than with the noise and poisons of the big city. Everyone should be so lucky to find that happy ending.

Isabelle Eberhardt's biographical writings and thinly veiled fictions based on her life in the desert and a simultaneously epic and melancholy view of the world's beauty and horror, illustrate another individual trying to both survive in the world and find a place in it that feels like "home." Like the Japanese poet Basho who wrote "the journey is home," Eberhardt seems to suggest that the most appropriate way to approach life is by recognizing that we are all wanderers and seekers and that wherever we find ourselves is what is meant to be.

The world exists as it does because language has been used by those who know how to use it to shape the world into the form they most want it to be.

Is the world the way you want it to be? Program your own channel. Make your own films. Publish your own books. Travel the world. Produce more than you consume.

We need to return one day to space and the stars, not just to find out what is out there, but because *out there* is where it's at.

Don't let your imagination become cynical just because you think everything's been done before. YOU haven't done it yet. Lethargy is for the others. It's not "all good." It needs to be better. Be a visionary.

TEST QUESTIONS (ESSAY FORMAT)

Strange new times ahead: describe them.

Write a short film about today (include soundtrack and specific cinematic details).

Write a short story about someone going to graduate school.

Describe the recent "angels" you have met.

Describe how television has improved your reality.

Write a short story about the most pleasant way to be unproductive.

Describe the love that you will soon embrace with the same emotion you describe a love that got away.

Write song titles for an imaginary album for a friend or stranger who acknowledged you in some way today (12 song titles. Include album title and cover art).

Explain your vision of the future.

Write a tale about the good life.

Write about the best meal you ever had & the best meal you will ever have in the future.

Write an essay about writing in response to an essay in this book.